SAY
I
DO
THIS

By the same author

Poetry
Whether the Will is Free
Crossing the Bar
Quesada
Walking Westward
Geographies
Poems of a Decade
Paris
Between
Voices
Straw into Gold
The Right Thing
Dog
The Red Tram
The Black River
Collected Poems, 1951–2006
The Yellow Buoy: Poems 2007–2012
In the Mirror, and Dancing
That Derrida Whom I Derided Died:
    Poems 2013–2017

Fiction
Smith's Dream
Five for the Symbol (stories)
All Visitors Ashore
The Death of the Body
Sister Hollywood
The End of the Century
    at the End of the World
The Singing Whakapapa
Villa Vittoria
The Blind Blonde with
    Candles in her Hair (stories)
Talking about O'Dwyer
The Secret History of Modernism
Mansfield
My Name Was Judas
Risk
The Name on the Door
    is Not Mine (stories)
The Necessary Angel

Memoir
South-West of Eden:
    A Memoir 1932–1956
You Have a Lot to Lose:
    A Memoir 1956–1986
What You Made of It:
    A Memoir 1987–2020

Criticism
The New Poetic
In the Glass Case
Pound, Yeats, Eliot
    and the Modernist Movement
Answering to the Language
The Writer at Work
Kin of Place: Essays on 20
    New Zealand Writers
Book Self: The Reader as Writer
    and the Writer as Critic
Shelf Life: Reviews, Replies
    and Reminiscences

Edited
Oxford New Zealand Short Stories
    (second series)
Measure for Measure, a Casebook
Letters and Journals
    of Katherine Mansfield
Collected Stories of Maurice Duggan
Faber Book of Contemporary
    South Pacific Stories
Werner Forman's New Zealand

SAY
I
DO
THIS

C. K. STEAD

POEMS 2018–2022

AUCKLAND
UNIVERSITY
PRESS

First published 2023
Auckland University Press
University of Auckland
Private Bag 92019
Auckland 1142
New Zealand
www.aucklanduniversitypress.co.nz

ISBN 978 1 77671 099 7

A catalogue record for this book is available from the
National Library of New Zealand

Design by Greg Simpson
This book was printed on FSC® certified paper
Printed in Singapore by Markono Print Media Pte Ltd

For Kay

'Just when the gods had ceased to be and the Christ had not yet come, there was a unique moment in history, between Cicero and Marcus Aurelius, when man stood alone. Nowhere else do we find that grandeur.'
　　 – **Gustave Flaubert**

'I know that half the audience might not understand this but I'm writing for the other half.'
　　 – **Tom Stoppard**

'so long / as there's a next, there's no last.'
　　 – **Allen Curnow**

'It is hard to renounce life once one is fond of it.'
　　 – **Ludwig Wittgenstein**

Contents

2. Away

3. … and Friends

1. Home

To be continued, perhaps

Horace, *Odes* I, 11

It's said that to know too much
displeases the gods, so for their sake, my love
stop asking for the end of our story:

no horoscopes, no animal entrails,
forget weather gurus in this time
of storms and climate disasters;

don't think of the waves at their worst
smashing on the rocks at Karekare
but share with me a bottle of Te Mata red.

We'll leave our grapevine and plum tree
to blackbird and thrush and other
untidy feeders, and to the wasps.

Let's talk together not about flashy Love
but the brilliant books and poems it has inspired
and the ones who wrote them –

brainy gossip, and jokes about the times
when there were still flowers to be picked.
Forget tomorrow my love. Just live with me today.

Tohunga Crescent

Across the street the Allen Curnow house
sold and garden-tidied and refurbished,
respectably letting as Airbnb

is home to wild parties, and just once
a riot bringing cop cars, a paddy wagon,
pepper spray and more than one arrest.

Always there's rubbish at the roadside when
the random tenants leave. Tonight by morepork
and moonlight while the neighbour cats patrol

I'm watching Jeny walk in her ghostly gown
smiling and weeping, and here comes Allen alert
with a new poem needing to know at once

what I will make of it – but as I read
he seems to slide away among the trees
all darkness and displeasure. There's a light

down at the Bay – that's Graham with his spear,
full tide at midnight, and the water still
holding itself for something new to reflect.

Morning will disclose the pōhutukawa
know it's December, time for spectacular blossom –
but Jeny's ambiguous tears have left me anxious

about those flashing lines of Allen light
seen and forgotten like the spell of weather
just gone you hadn't known might be a blessing.

Ode to Autumn

This day's officially the first of autumn
but it seems not to know.
The sun's all over everything and the sea
flinches and glitters.
We've shared our plums with thrush and blackbird
but the rules are beyond them
and they're destroying the grapes.
Still I won't use the nets –
too much trouble, too many casualties.
'Altruism' – that's the word Antonia made
the last thought of her character who dies
saving the life of a sparrow.
Today's flowers are blue –
lasiandra, agapanthus
and the violet morning glory
vivid on a bank above mangroves.
I watch the tide
breathe in over the mud-flats.
A high-stepping heron stops a moment
then flaps off languidly on elegant wings.
'We are so lucky' someone reflects
down at the Bay – and so we are I suppose.
I lead a life of quiet medication
longing for foreign shores, adventure and death.

On a day late summer in a poem like wine

I ask what it's like out there and she replies
'Gorgeous – "like silk" to quote your lovely poem.'

She must be third or fourth to tell me that –
so I'm known here as a poet, and for a line

that says the water out at the yellow buoy
on a good day feels like silk. For that nice trope

I'm 'famous at Kohi' – but neither my recall
nor my books seem to confirm I wrote it.

Today's one of those rare and windless ones,
the surface all the way to Rangitoto

glassy, while the water that's been tepid
now has a hint of winter, making it feel

indeed like *silk!* – so I catch up with myself
on a day late summer in a poem like wine.

Pastoral: Kaiwaka, 1941

Cruelly raped, Mrs Housefly shakes herself,
seems to wash her hands and dry her eyes,

then soldiers on with duties of full summer –
goodies to sample, important eggs to be laid.

She has not read her Shakespeare so doesn't know
of Lear's distress that 'wren and gilded fly

do lecher in my sight'. She has no idea
of her bad press, nor that in one high corner

Sir Spider is composing a web of lies
to capture her or (he can wait) her children.

Out in the yard a boy sits bareback astride
the horse he rides to the gate for mail and meat,

a 9-year-old, doing his 'Bing' or his 'Frank'.
Heifers lift ruffled brows as he sings by.

Say I do this

Say I tell the accountant who does my tax,
or the IRD itself, that at eighty-nine

it's too hard to get the numberings correct –
too much fiddle. Say I make them an offer –

a thousand, two at most. I was recalling
our neighbour Dr André at Maunsell Road

when a small fragment of steel got in my eye –
it was the weekend, he'd been drinking, and I watched

his instrument waver towards my eye – and stop.
'Don't *move*' he said, loud, as if he meant it. Later

we had whiskey with Father Forsman looking out
on Pasifika kids playing in his school yard.

'My Aegean Greeks' he said, thinking of the War.
One K should do it. I've made fuck all this year.

Dombey & Son

Predation and defections had reduced
the family in the loft to two – both male
so we gave them story names, Dombey & Son.

They lived on roofs and ranged about the gully
down to the Bay and beyond, but always
back on time for feeding and to sleep.

When the sun was hot they sheltered in an alcove
under Tracy Moresby's eaves, and listened to
Tracy, an old gay man, play Schubert and Brahms.

It was the cat called Zac-the-Knife who caught
Dombey in a drain and clawed his throat.
Wings undamaged, he flew first to the loft

and then, with Son, made it all the way
to Tracy's alcove, and never moved again.
Every day Son would call on him

and, walking up and down, relay the news
of roofs and gully, the Bay, and even beyond
to the dead Dombey. Dutiful, never failing

through autumn, winter, until – October it was
Son found himself a mate and joined the defectors.
The loft, empty, derelict, we demolished

but up there still old Tracy Moresby played
Schubert and Brahms to a corpse with white feathers
rippling and ruffling in the breeze of spring.

To 'Amnesia,
Muse of Deletions'

Swimming in the dark I call on memory –
        Rangitoto ahead, and those lights
              of Kohi behind making

a cosy half-circle. Overhead the moon's
        a waka sailing west to escape
              first light that will put it out.

I'm reaching blind fingers for the yellow buoy
        and touch it only as the sun does
              dimly through a bank of cloud

remembering Allen's 'Blind Man's Holiday'
        and our exchange about it. His God
              smelled of laundered linen, mine

(though I didn't have one) of mānuka – but
        a whiff from the Kohi Café of
              breakfast bacon has a hint

of the divine. I'd argued that a poem
        couldn't do pain and he'd thought that might
              be right but gave it a shot –

his ride by ambulance from Lone Kauri Road
        through St Lukes, gulping gas and pleading
              'How much longer?' – but learning

the anaesthetic wisdom that erases
        the searing moment too hot ever
              to be held. Allen is dead

but not his poem, and I remember Lawrence
　　Durrell saying that dying 'makes you
　　　　out of date but brings your chums

to their senses'. Tomorrow, first-light swimming
　　I'll ask them both at the yellow buoy
　　　　do the dead forget their friends?

Mary

The first time I saw her
three children, seven grandchildren and how many cats
ago
she was 20, a student in a bathing suit, hosed
on the front lawn by her mother.
We were buying the house next door, number 37.
The last time she was old, naked on her bathroom floor
mumbling, unconscious. She may have been there two days.
Death took a further four. There were no 'last words'.

They were a Trinity, Mother, Daughter and Roy
the Holy Ghost. I carried Roy to the ambulance
for his last ride. Zoe lived on,
played golf and bridge, died in an old folks' home
and not a thing at number 39
was changed – the interiors forever Zoe's,
the garden Roy's. Was Mary their resentful prisoner
or just a loyal daughter?

Travelling we always sent her a postcard
of a new exotic corner. She kept them all,
also my glowing reference supporting
her application for her first job.
When she retired she was HOD Art
at the same college.

Mary always seemed too tough for tears:
those who'd loved her were with her – Zoe whose yellow car
she kept in running order, Roy whose lawns she mowed
and flower-beds she replanted.

When we talked it was about the weather
and what was happening in Tohunga Crescent;
her decades teaching seemed to have floated away.
She walked the Bonnys' dog, had drinks with them,
went to a gym, had Christmas with her cousins.
In her chest of drawers were found
new dresses still shop-wrapped, 'outfits' never worn –
it seemed she'd liked shopping. Sometimes
she borrowed a book from us. There was one she liked
by Jim McNeish about Oxford and spies.
I promised I would tell her more about Mulgan . . .

All those years of the world behaving badly –
how much of it touched her?
And yet she's there still,
the stylish, busy, never-subdued Mary
who borrowed my garden tools
and tended (cheerfully) to shout
in conversation.
The silent house next door is full of her,
full of her absence.

＊

It was not the Ides of March;
the virgin Mary lacked significance
without a Son. Where was the turbulence,
the black sky torn across?
She was in her box but hadn't she been there always
elusive, undeclared? A neighbour poet
(not this one) had written her
a kindly dirge. So we went through the motions
and out the door, and she into the fire.

Days later swimming with my friend Geoff
at Kohi we met a whale at the yellow buoy.
It circled us, listening to our talk
and followed us inshore.
Geoff stroked its flank. It was a visitation,
Nature giving us a call
on the right side of silence:
alpha, omega, a poem, and Mary forgetting.

The corner

I'd come past that corner where the big white wooden house
(gone now, like the girl herself)
had framed her fantasy of a smart apartment
where our being, hers and mine, might merge right back
into another beginning. The Scented Garden for the Blind,
our place of parting, that too was gone.
Change it's called. 'Just go for god's sake!' it says,
and one yields to it, and fails and fades
into that good night.

Hobson Bay

Judging by the number of stabs
Pūkeko's quarry are more numerous than Heron's.
Is she just an undiscriminating chook
with her flicking white tail-feathers and proletarian feet:
'Anything moves, *I eat it!*'
Certainly Heron is more elegant
and seems fastidious –
our aristocrat.

Soon will come the godwits and other migrators
for their few days' R & R before flying
twelve thousand kms!
Regular, dependable, enduring, even through the long decades
of the Cold War they took up residence
on this side then on far-side
ruled only by the seasons and their genes,
ignorant of the Red Menace, the American Eagle
the threat of nuclear war and nuclear meltdown
and climate change –
just spies, that's all, with secret intelligence
of wind and water.

Waking in a Time of Trouble

The 42-year-old in the supermarket
stabs one of the assistants
and then another.
Courageous colleagues wrestle him to the floor
hold him down with a chair
and call the cops.
Maybe he's mad or high on P – who knows? –
but he wears a T-shirt that says
SONS OF ANARCHY
while in the same town
students are resisting moves to clear their streets
of abandoned sofas
bags of outgrown clothes
and bad old shoes.
The cold front scattering
snow on those autumn hills
will reach us here as hail
and I wake in pieces
feeling I must have been
in the thick of it, one of the wounded perhaps
or even (could I have been?) the knifeman
hustled handcuffed, buffeted to a cell
and now to answer the charge.
'Not guilty (your honour)' I hear myself murmur
but the voice may not be mine
and sounds uncertain.

Haiku: Audiology

In the blackbirds' calls
you can often distinguish
phrases, usually

English but French too.
German and Māori can be
distinguished sometimes.

I've heard 'Mozart' and
even 'Tūrangawaewae'
and just once I caught

'das heilige Kind'
meaning of course the Baby
born in a manger –

often religious
and sometimes tending to preach.
If your hearing's less

than perfect your wife
may seem to 'speak in tongues'. Mine
warned me the Bible's

not to be trusted
even at the best of times
which these are not. Once

after swimming I
heard an immunologist
quoting lines about

a fisherman dressed
'in grey Connemara cloth' –
Yeats of course. I was

impressed and so was
Jim Mora. What tūī have
to say is never

uninteresting
but pigeons are given to
self-repetition.

'Audible' they say,
'Audible' and how you wish
it wasn't. And then

'Oracle' which might
be a brand signalling their
internet server.

Then there's cicada
tinnitus making each day
'one summer's' as if

the start of a short
story. When I was a boy
people were not so

well-informed; now the
air's full of Keats quotations,
snatches of Shakespeare,

Eliot and Donne.
On a bus once I heard 'the
long withdrawing roar'

– that's Matthew Arnold's
'Sea of Faith' and how despite
Lockdown rules it's still

going out. The birds
it seems know just what's going
on and it's not good.

Haiku

My forebear's lost grave
is found in Te Aroha
close to the racecourse.

Now a plaque will show
John Flatt 1805 to
the century's end.

So catechist John
let us agree to donate
our smidgen of fame

each to the other –
yours for truths told and mine for
writing about them.

Just Checking

Elizabeth Smither's
poem tells me
that the heart

repairs between
beats. Checking on
mine at 3 a.m.

I register
48 per minute
with the odd

one missed. I
slip back into sleep
dreaming that the staff,

students, buildings,
the university –
or is that

the Universe?
(and of course
it is) depend upon

this solo organ
steady for the moment
while I

still with numb
fingers numbering
at my throat recall

time's winged chariot
at Marvell's back
telling him to

remind his girl
that in the grave
there's no embracing.

This side of silence

When her sparrow brushed
                    my Clodia's lips
he gave her the gift of happiness
                    which she gave me –
never mind the turbulence
        the contradictions and conflict
this was aroha.

Now Orcus has taken them both
                    into his Nowhere
and Catullus in his old-man face
                    has time to tell himself
'The world as you found it my friend
                    was neither
                        benign nor malign
but what you made of it.

            So here at last, at the last
            your voice hardly more than
                a wind among reeds
remember
you are still this side of silence:
                    make the most of it.'

Birthday Tercets for Kay

24/12/2018

I woke wondering
        how I might wish you
                happy eighty-

fifth in the
        language of the
                tangata whenua

and could not,
        te reo Māori being
                one of those things

not learned in this
        life, like Separation
                which must happen

because even should
        we die together
                (plane crash or the

Oregon Out) you will
        not be with me
                in the Big Dark

and I will not
        be myself, I will be
                Nothing. So I

imagined a morning
    when we are
        up just after first

light before the first
    wind when the
        sea beyond Kohi is

glass all the way
    out past Rangitoto
        to Waiheke

and send you on
    your birthday in
        te reo Pākehā

one swim in our
    only heaven, which comes
        with all my love.

Anonymity and Silence

My first true love Diane (pronounced as in French)
told me when we parted, in love and in pain,
she'd like my 'poet's head' ('noble' she called it)

for ever on her bedpost. Was it to be
in sightless bronze or with these live eyes watching
as she and the one who followed me made love,

had children, grew together and grew apart,
prospered, played golf (she did not play) while the head
forgiving but not forgetting aged into

this wrinkled troll and she, Diane (as in France)
now widowed, that long-ago wish forgotten,
asked only for anonymity and silence.

Something to tell

I see it in motion
as in a movie
the thrush, wings wide in flight,
the cat leaping, stretching, high
one paw catching
and myself matching
grabbing a tight handful of cat
as paw hooks bird.

Pain and release –
the thrush flies free
and I, cat still in hand
crash to the deck
eighty-eight years of self in action
'doing good', 'saving a life'.

Now the cat sulks and won't be fed.
I nurse bruised knees
and pulled calf muscle
pleased with myself
looking for someone to tell.

After surgery

One eye shows me a less-than-perfect world;
a dear one's imprecations hang over us both.
In hours of least light I hear my heart
walking with a stick and knocking into things.
Death will be not unwelcome though I'd hoped
for a friendlier exit. A dream delivers me
home south-west of Eden. I hunt for my chooks,
feed them and give them water. My Dad's bean-rows
are green, Mum is at her piano, Nana's reading
about the stars and big sister's bossy. I
am ten years old and we are winning the war.

To any gardener with a terminal prognosis

Garden as always
according to time of year
as if the seasons
and your garden's responses
('World without end')
will be the same –
as you have to hope they will be
even without you.

Poem in October

(with shades of Dylan Thomas)

It was my ninetieth year to heaven
woke to my hearing from Hobson Bay neighbourhood
signals of early fruit on grapevine and plum tree
and down on the mud-flats our migrant seabirds returning
while in nearby gardens blackbird and thrush were harassed
from nests in carport and hedge by their thankless offspring,
my morning walk
to take me abroad in a shower of all my days –
Becoming, Being, and then Fading
thirty years each, but the Becoming had been slow
('Don't peak too early') and overlapped with Being
as Being slid into the Fade.

It was the Wintergarden glasshouses taught
what Gaea might make of moisture and of heat
such flowers and leaves, extravagance of colour
a dance, an abundance of vividness and texture
Colombian, Amazonian
and scent, and size! Global warming it seemed
might be beautiful if that meant anything
with few or none of us human left to watch
its vegetable amplitude, its fires and floods
and tooth and claw.

At ease around ponds the daffodils praised Wordsworth
and trees in imperial uniform saluted
while up on the hill a Cenotaph and guns
told us a war had made us what we were
and bound us together. I used to walk there
after a day at work to look down at the port

and across North Shore and out beyond Rangitoto
hungry for another taste not – no not at all
of war but of the world.
It was a happy place, a space in my head
where Heaney and Heidegger could argue over God
while I looked out and listened or didn't listen
to the city's indignant rumour
and thought about Zen and how it might conjoin
mind and matter into the shapes and movement
of the atom, but also of the stars.

It was my ninetieth year to heaven
and the weather turned around
only a pale grey cloud and a pearly shower
but I saw in the turning so clearly
a boy's visits to that place climbing with his sister
on the guns and hearing how great-uncle Owen
would 'grow not old' (a mysterious locution)
because at the going down of the sun and in the morning
a brass plaque would remember him who 'Died
for Freedom and Honour'.

It was the first day of my ninetieth year
stood there then in the promise of another summer
the English trees reforming in October green
knowing that humanity was no more than another
passing thought, a brainstorm of Gaea our mother
all-powerful and lovely and now demanding a cull.
No I did not want these hard truths still to need telling
on that small hill in a year's turning
nor forgiveness for past mistakes but only to say to my world
'Kia ora for having me. Stay safe. Go well.'

2. Away

What Next?

Pictures of Russell Square – its big green summer,
technicolour autumn, and the grand old Hotel Russell

seen through black sticks of winter – and looking west
wasn't that the Senate House looming? It was then I saw

that though I knew I'd never see London again
I hadn't known what I knew – not the BM steps

where I'd conjured a prize-winning poem, not the River
and all its bridges, not Paddington, not Queen's Park –

and time to say my goodbyes to Hammersmith . . .
It could have been a moment of real regret

and tearful verse – but it brought me to this page
to say 'OK that's done, so what comes next?' –

never mind you know quite well there is no Next,
that next is Nothing. Lean into it, as into a wind.

The Death of Orpheus

The death of Orpheus was an unpleasantness
of blood and bone, but the music did not die.

The head that women loved, by women severed
floated downstream to sea, and came to Lesbos.

The hands were gone so it must have been the wind
that played his lyre, and the bruised mouth still sang.

It's said on falling leaves were lyric texts
that looked past winter and remembered well

the wife he lost in the rear-vision mirror.
The birds joined in, and streams too, rehearsing

songs the youthful poet made in spring.
If there should be much more of us than shadow

and a name, then yes, in some Elysian valley
Orpheus lives, and sings, and his songs are heard.

Proses

1.

Did she want it down on paper? There were those poems
of the nineteen-fifties used to begin with scenery
and end with ethics, passing by way of the weather
as now for example the humid spring has darkened
and turned to rain. Reflection on reflections of
reflections, like the green leaves in a mirror
held over still water, a memory out of childhood
gently merging into the knowledge of loss. How they
did go on the voices of the virtues of our fathers
and of their sons, and the last word going down
out of the failing light into this rain still falling
on the suburb of our wishing – it was always love.

2.

If you come upon me in the fields please behave
naturally. There's no miracle like Stendhal's mirror
and the boot can't always have been on the other foot.

3.

Holding it high the priest in starched parchment presents
Christ with a silver cup for the best sportsman of the
year. The effigy looks down and cannot accept it. He
supports the east wall. Subdued by the ineffable, the
indulgent, I pad out pursued by an anthem. Grass is
green, graves grey and greyer, a thatched pub all beams
and brass is open to the sun. A branch line has burst
into leaf. Nothing is exactly vertical or horizontal,
nothing unpardonable. A Sunday newsboard announces
a new tax on cigarettes. Is this new? Undeterred I light one.
In ancient Rome one might have known how to behave.
Where is the world? Where are the keys to my car?

Movie review: *The Misfits*

Directed by John Huston, script by Arthur Miller,
with Marilyn Monroe, Clark Gable and Montgomery Clift

She screams at them 'You are liars, killers, dead men.'
They rope the mustang and fight it to the ground.

It's a kind of sport although there's money in it –
less profit than pride, and now the blonde hates them.

Still screaming in her rage she's beautiful,
but sentimental, a girl in love with horses.

They haven't heard, and neither has she, of Nietzsche
weeping, hugging a cart-horse in Turin;

nor of Raskolnikov's forewarning dream –
a horse beaten to death; nor of this boy

on the family farm seeing an angry cousin
whipping his old tired mount to make her gallop:

men and horses, cowboys and weeping blondes –
more than all that, it was about compassion.

'At the Bay'

Montaigne thought we were going to bless the future
                    but it was the past she wanted to bless –
                        the mother surprised by love
for her unintended baby
            the Pa-man's pain and self-regard and bluster,
the promise the grandmother knitting could not make,
            the hollow voice of the uncle seeing himself
                        as an insect trapped in a room
of inkpots and wire blinds,
and the young auntie's moonlit vision on the veranda
                            and over the lawn
to the dark pit under the fuchsia
that was life – or was it death?

David Mitchell in Menton

Here you were
in the Memorial Room
where you'd so much wanted to be,
out there the trains stopping at Garavan
or going by into Italy
and the ghost girl reading in the little garden
or calling from the deck above 'Hello' to Jack
while time consumed itself waiting
for your next good word, your next clean line.

You'd never learned to ask
not 'nicely', that wasn't the problem
but in the language of the truly deserving –
with authority.

So here you were then
and nothing, no one not even your lovely Elizabeth
had seemed to lean on you with so much weight,
such sense of a debt of thanks waiting to be paid
where the sea was blue all the way out
to the blue of the sky
and the food was French, and the language
the language of poetry,
and you writing still of a world
'at odds with the dreamer but at one with the dream'
while everything fell apart and panicked around you
and the grey-orange rock-faces of the Alpes Maritimes
glared down like clowns in masks demanding
'Dave, why are you here?'

Côte d'Azur

Waiting for a bus
on the Menton
seafront I met

my late friend Mike.
He'd walked some distance
looked dusty and

somehow reduced
by decease. We
resolved to meet for

a meal we both
knew not possible
and hugged goodbye.

'Love ya Bro' was
something I'd say
only in a dream

he shedding (likewise)
a tear. My bus
would take me to

the airport at
Nice a window seat
all in sight of

that heart-wrenching
coast where our kids
are forever small

myself packed up
for check-in and the
flight to Nowhere.

Sonnet in a time of Lockdown

Longing for one last taste of the Côte d'Azur
I'm reading poet Cavafy who perhaps

was never there but in a place just like it –
same vines and olives, cafés and crooked streets

and cheap hotels, he remembering sadly
a lover's body, savour of skin and hair,

the same sea's breath fresh from an open window,
and he at his wits' end now, writing of age

and ugliness that came unwelcome upon him
like wounds from a cruel knife. So, as when

the god (or luck) forsook Mark Antony
he turned his back on Alexandria,

you too Cavafy hid and shunned your friends
not wanting your less-than-beauty to be seen.

October 16, 1817,
Angostura, 5 p.m.

A gold carriage and carnage
                              were never far apart
so when the bravest General
in the fight against Spain
                    called on the Mestizos to rise up
                              against white privilege
his death was assured.

A dog devoured by buzzards was removed
from the town square:
                    the hero must die in public.

As the gunshots echoed
                    from the Cathedral walls
                              Bolívar wept
                              and told his servant
'That's my own blood I've shed.'

The Dream of Carlos Amigo

She's telling me (I think)
that she can't live without me.
I feel the love
but lack the language.
In the white Cathedral
with windows depicting pain
seven priests in green burn incense
at their magic table
and intone
for us on our marble knees.
In the Bolívarian Square
drunks and addicts sleep
under the widespread wings
of waiting condors.
A dead dog swivels
in the brown river
and a growl of thunder
utters from the mountains.
I don't want to say 'Adiós'
but a prostate nearing ninety
is more urgent even than love
and the love of God.
Did she have a name?
Mine was Carlos Amigo.

Sonnet: Paula Rego and an inn

What was it Paula saw that day she heard
the name 'Miranda' and the poem about her
remembering (or not – that was the question)
an inn – and Kay and I watching the painter
with her best man-model and a peasant woman
and her stuffed dolls and the cherry-picker hired
to hoist her up to paint her tallest canvas
with its tales of tortured women and girls raped.

Remembering together we recited
that poem for her and for her Anthony
the faithful love who'd call her night after night
so they could have it again, the inn, the fleas,
the Pyrenees, the wine that tasted of the tar,
and Portugal and childhood and perhaps lost love.

The thousand peaceful towns

for the lady herself

It was meant to show when 'l' sounded as 'l'
and not as 'y'. English but fluent in French,

a Paris professor, surely she'd heard it?
But as a way of rhyme-remembering

like a tale of travel in a time of peace –
no, she hadn't. I was showing off of course.

I'd quoted Paul Verlaine's lachrymose sonnet
about the phantom woman who dried his tears.

'Brune, blonde ou rousse?' he asks himself, quite sure
only that her voice was lovely – 'doux et sonore'.

I was pleased with myself for giving his mute 'e's
the full value those alexandrines needed

to make the iambic count. Was she impressed?
Not really. She probably thought I was flirting.

Fin

There was ice on the pond
beyond the willows, and when
the whole world went quiet
I knew the forecast snow had begun to fall.
She was old, and dying, and had never seen it
she said (which I didn't believe)
except in movies. So I went out into the night
and brought her back a small ball of it
and put it into her cupped hands
where together we watched it melt.

Impromptu: Afghanistan

Three thousand troops are sent in
to pull the diplomats out –
Vietnam again
another well-meant intrusion
turns to disaster.

Stronger than ever
the Bad Guys are winning
while at home your citizens, America
turn guns they claim as a constitutional right
on one another.

Last night I saw
bright Pointers and a fainter Southern Cross
sharing our velvet sky
with the waning moon
while somewhere a radio played
smooth Dino crooning
    'Everybody
    loves somebody
    sometime'.

America we love you
(sometimes) but
why so daft, so thick
so unwilling to learn?

Psalms of Judas, 1

This morning
scanning the sky out beyond the islands
I remembered my friend's eyes cast heavenward
for the chariot of angels
that would carry him home
and how he cried out in pain to his father
asking why he had been forsaken;

and I thanked Reason
and our tutor Andreas
whose Greek wisdom had released me
from the Religion that wished death
upon the daughters of Babylon
and that their little ones
should be dashed on the stones.

Then as now there was no cloud of angels
no choir-in-the-sky
no miracle, but only his pain and his death
and an end to magic.
So I live with Chance under a sky
that visits what it will upon me
knowing that I too must die.

But still there is prayer
to those imagined Powers
whose playthings and instruments
we suppose we are,
and under willows where
we pitch our tents and hang our harps at evening,
the songs of Zion.

Psalms of Judas, 2

I am old now, three score and ten
but remember his eloquence
like running water
that shone and sparkled catching the light
and there was silence in it
and darkness – so magic
happened, or seemed to.

Language was the power,
it filled the vats his mother insisted
were empty of wedding wine;
it made the dying Lazarus
come back who had heard
the angel choirs
and seen a farther shore.

It seemed to speak true
and made the fishermen cast their nets
where they knew were no fish
yet wasn't the catch a record?
So they believed he was divine
as I did not. Disbelief –
that was my talent, my betrayal.

Psalms of Judas, 3

When we were boys
and played together, and sometimes fought
his mother told me
I was too clever by half;
I didn't know what she meant.
Her eyes held on to their secret
like a stone in a stream.

He was the golden one
she never reproached or smacked
though she kept a stick
for the ones who came after.
He was cool with her;
asked her 'Woman
what have I to do with you?'

Only in John's report
was she there at the end.
It was his father
he cried out to
looking always to the skies
that remained blue and blank
and indifferent to pain.

Psalms of Judas, 4

He was not my shepherd
nor did I want one.
As boys we camped in green pastures
beside still waters
which restored our souls.

He could have come with me to Greece
where goodness and mercy
and reason reign;
or gone with Mary Magdalene
who loved him not as a god
but as a man.

But Jerusalem called
and eloquence and power.
He chose to live by his story
and die by it,
my brilliant friend
nailed to a cross.

The challenge

15 April 2019

Notre-Dame is burning. Science detects
a Black Hole at the outer edge of space.
The spire falls. Nothing taught in that place

has ever been confirmed – no god, no devil,
no heaven, no hell, no afterlife revealed.
In outer space a Black Hole long concealed

by distance, tells us science gets it right.
Prayers go unanswered and a Christian learns
his God is silent while Our Lady burns.

National Anthems

16 June (Bloomsday) 2021

Philip Matthews says
Stead feels more at home
in France than

in Wellington. My
friend Tony who
has lived in both

asks 'Who wouldn't?'
Maria Stepanova
tells her friend

Sasha that her poems
are an attempt
to love her

country 'because
someone has to'.
Borges wished to die

in Geneva
which was 'nice and
not Argentina'.

Joyce chose Zurich,
Pound Venice, because
they were neither

Ireland nor the
US. Eliot
preferred England,

Stevenson
Vailima in Samoa,
both far from

home and loyalty
to flag. It seems
I must pay my

country the respect
of dying right here
but only

(honours to the
pandemic)
because of the Lockdown.

3. ...and Friends

Poem for Kevin

after reading Keeping a Grip

A cup of rice and two of water
bring to the boil and simmer
while you slice the big red onions
to fry in oil with bacon, sliced small or diced.

When the rice is right mix all in the big pan
adding mussels and oysters
(the small ones in tins are fine)
and stir – with pepper of course. And no, Kevin

bugger the Lemora – no need
to be slavish. It's time the sons of Sargeson
taught him about wines – we'll have
the chardonnay. Now taste, and Hey Presto!

aren't we back in our wizard's Fibro cave
talking books and writers, hearing the old magician
holding forth, holding out against
this word-poor witless *fuck of a world?*

Thelma

After six decades an overseas call from
Fred Foulds misses me. 'No worries' he tells Kay,
he'd 'only wanted to know Stead wasn't dead'.

Fred was our national chess champ whose Kodak caught
my younger self in Fair Isle smoking a pipe.
I could have told him that Jean and Les were dead,

and last month Barry, another of our friends.
Google tells me Thelma our red-haired dancer
teacher of French (retired) has died in Portsmouth.

Back then I listened to her seventy-eights
of Stephen Spender poems and took her dancing
at the Civic Wintergarden Cabaret.

We were Travolta and Thurman, Torvill and Dean –
the ease, the grace that gives to music a body.
Thelma and I didn't 'make love'. We danced.

For Jane Massey

in the manner of Horace

What was it pulled me down to Stygian deeps
then changed its mind and made Apollo wait?

It was the thought of something still to write
for her upon the shore. Hear me O Seas

and star-bright Skies, how could I give up the ghost
when Jane had ordered I should not forget

her *fiftieth!* Mother, lawyer and wit
whose voice commands, here I struggle ashore

breathless and weak, but thanking you for life,
honouring your years and wishing you fifty more.

For Fleur Adcock

You teach us how many poems are hiding
in a small precinct, in the short circuit
of a garden close to a wood –
how many small animals, insects and birds
with their quirks, their colours and behaviours –
never mind memory that other octogenarian
storehouse and stumbling-block
for the sensibility that lives at the last by language
and the gifts of friendship
and may die alone leaving the front door open.

MacSpaunday

They were quite posh –
name of Margitson.
He was MI6
later a diplomat
and knighted –
colleague and friend of John le Carré
whose real name was Cornwell.
His mother-in-law Nancy
who'd had an affair
with Louis MacNeice
was married first to the painter Coldstream,
then to a Spender –
the one killed in the War.
She was the one
left her baby
to be looked after briefly
by their lodger Auden
and came home to find him
with the baby at his breast?
Wystan said it had kept the child quiet
and taught him what it was like
to be a mother.

To John Berryman

Well met by moonlight, friend
to the sound of these shimmering
Mendelssohn strings.

'Laziness, liquor, bad dreams' –
I suffered somewhat from each
but not like you
they drove to that bridge
on Washington Avenue
and off it. 'We all die' you said,
'and after? The evidence is Nothing.'

Will I be here tomorrow?
I don't know but I'd like to be.

The big white bears
and the yellow-eyed penguins
are heading for extinction,
and the dead in heaven
or wherever they pass their fade
must be aware at least
of becoming insubstantial.

'The thing meanwhile' you said
'is to be courageous and kind.'

13-syllable tercets on behalf of Goats

and for Jo Emeney

Don't tether your goat
    all alone to trim
        your roadside.

Give her a friend and
    talk to her or
        she'll be depressed.

Put an open
    hand to her brow
        for a push-of-war.

Not good to goats
    the Bible God
        separates them from

favoured sheep that
    they may be scapegoats
        stoned for our sins.

I prefer to give
    thought to Capricorn
        who suckled

Zeus destined
    for top godship on
        Mount Olympus.

Then there's Pan
        half-goat half-man
                who in Arcadia

plays his pipe to
        fields and forest glens
                and running streams

inspiring shepherds
        with dreams of
                beautiful women.

Picasso's sculpted
        goat was once two
                ceramic jugs,

one wicker basket,
        scrap wire, palm fronds
                and vine-wood horns –

but there's a shot
        of a young goat
                asleep on his lap.

Warned of the wolf
        but craving free air
                and the mountains

Daudet's brave goat
        escaped and is
                honoured in Provence

for her night-long
    fight lost only as
        the sun came up.

In this shot Jo
    and her goat Rosie
        are conversing

about Daudet
    Darwin and the kinship
        of species –

but there's a smiling
    one, both saying 'Cheese'
        (goat of course).

Murnane Country

'Perhaps I wrote in order to provide myself with the equivalent in the invisible world of Tasmania and New Zealand in the visible world.'
   – Gerald Murnane

Neither inane nor murky but somewhat of both
and not to be confused with north-of-the-Arctic Circle Murmansk
it is a landscape of landscapes
in the head of a man once but no longer Catholic
silent in a very large bar
who can neither taste his beer nor imagine its taste –
a region of racetracks
with more grass than all of Australia together
and grazed by a small marsupial lately lost
in which every horse may be Phar Lap
and any jockey a winner of the Melbourne Cup.

You may look at this man-in-the-moon man as he may look at you
who was named after his father's best galloper and believes
all art aspires to the condition of horseracing –
but do not engage, do not lock eyes with him
who likes freckled women more than the gold or the beige
on satin cushions and in marble bathrooms,
preferring the one with imperfect skin
who takes him by the hand to a wide back window looking out
on a landscape like Dandenong where he might live for ever
going always and ever nowhere
drinking and thinking and filling his nineteen filing cabinets
with the writings of one like himself.

Keep him in mind who may be nobbled and
riding for a fall
or worth a few dollars for a place.

A Sonnet ending on a note of uncertainty

It was Seamus told the story of
the Russian poet at that darkest time

of Stalin's terror burying his work
in glass preserving jars in his garden

at night for safety, the scene preserving
an Irish flavour – secrets and the sense

of history as a force for truth that would
rise up in later years and tell its tale,

the dictator's nightmare – but more than that
a challenge to anyone who compromised

to earn rewards. The scene was Oxford and
the biggest prize still waiting to be won.

Did he hesitate just once, was there even
the faintest tremor in that famous voice?

Keri Hulme – *The Bone People*

Think of the violence first, the pain
inflicted on the child and then

the love all round and back again
the circle Keri made and how

it grew and gave her fortune, fame
a debt called 'Bait' she could not pay,

a promise always unfulfilled.
In Ōkārito's whitebait season

which is a kind of keen unreason
'Keri is dead' that coastline cries

incarnadining pastel skies.
The boy, the man who beats him still,

the bragging woman, the brutal shore
make sense of these and tell the world

how latitude and boozy glory
combined to make her once-and-ever

the never-back-again front runner,
the dark compelling neuter story.

Smalls

for Roger & Wystan

I was out to lunch when
Creeley called.
It was raining.
He left me one white
chicken-feather and a chip
off the old red
wheelbarrow.

Dreamed a billboard
reading FRANK O'HARA
HAS SOX APPEAL.
'You mean sex', was what
he said
lounging and laughing
among the sand dunes.

Had a Zen haircut with Gary
Snyder
and took off with him
for a stint of
hunting and burning.

Crossing the Bar

remembering the Thwaites

Ann and Anthony, Anthony and Ann
at Low Tharston, Norfolk punting on the mill stream
through reeds and the purple damselflies
                          of an English summer,
playing table tennis among the trees
or in winter under oaken beams
before a fire in the Mill House
                          being bookish together –

he the editor-poet famous for Larkin
(and sometime shaman of the Anglican communion)
she the biographer, archivist of secrets
                          and family matters
who bounced on their trampoline in the woods
telling me she couldn't write her life story
while Anthony lived –

                    and hadn't she been
my fantasy bossy little Pom
at the Mt Eden Pool of my childhood swims?

And then at the last Anthony, dying at 90
being read to by Ann
                    and watched by her –
he silent and seeming unconscious
while she was heard to say
                he might be 'crossing the horizon'
eliciting from the deathbed
that voice still Anthony's – 'the *BAR*'.

Even at the door
            one foot in another world
you must get your quotations right –
that was our Anthony
            on his way.

A sonnet for Peter Wells

At your last book launch I said I hadn't known
which of us would die first – and I still didn't.

We joked about sad farewells, but when I said
an atheist's last could not be 'See you later'

I thought your brow darkened – so I'm not surprised
your obsequies today were Anglican

with 'sure and certain hope' of resurrection.
How could poor weak 'hope' be 'sure and certain'?

but as your coffin ablaze with white blossom
was walked to the waiting hearse and trundled off

3 orcas entered the harbour, a trinity,
a Sign perhaps, Peter, and fond farewell

to one who as a boy had wanted a doll
and as a man found one, and married him.

Iris

We four senior professors (a Broederbond)
entertained John Bayley and Iris Murdoch
for dinner at the posh White Heron Motel

with dance-floor and band and lovely views out to
the Auckland Harbour. Bailey had lectured on
the M-Modern N-Novel, she on Sartre.

There was much talk, some stammering, and only
shy Forrest Scott was silent until quite late
he leaned to whisper something into her hair –

and she, surprised but smiling, answered 'Of course –
thank you' – and off they went. He whirled her away
first in a waltz, then in a sexy foxtrot.

Months later in the mail-room Forrest showed me
a card had come from her, now back in Oxford:
'Hello Foxxy Trot. Fondest greetings, Iris.'

Creative Writing Class: Syllabics

You tell me that in my novels the wife is
either absent or alien, and sometimes
a challenge. I argue that in those stories

you cannot be you nor can I be myself –
this not so much a rule as a preference
for distance. But there are likenesses – moments

'from life' and nothing that's ever reductive.
We are ourselves beyond realities of
Time and Space in a dream neither flower-filled

nor a stony road but (let's hope) credible.
The lilac you gave me is in full leaf and
I've named it Olive after my much-loved Mum.

Our grapevine makes promises it might not keep.
Gaea sends the plum tree an enamelled crop,
then a gale to blow most of it down. Her ways

you remind me are inscrutable. Swimming
at Kohimarama means summer's in sight,
and in Glasgow the leaders of the World are

redesigning it. No more novels – just this
with its hunger for eloquence and only
syllables to count on. And spring, and dying.

An encounter in Belsize Park Gardens

Grey hair, grey suit, blue tie, and on the lapel
a huge green brooch – this passing Indian asks
'Sir, Madame, could you spare a moment to talk?'

and the bloodshot eyes are suddenly full of tears.
'Talk … of course. Is there something … Are you unwell?'
He says, 'Thirty-five years I've lived in that flat …'

and stops. 'Evicted?' No. He tries to explain.
'I am not sure I exist. How can I know? –
thirty-five bloody years …' And again the tears.

There had been times … Just once he'd been in a lab
with Einstein. That was his year in Princeton.
Now he had no colleagues, no wife, no children,

but last night walking on Primrose Hill he'd seen
the moon's eclipse – marvellous, a miracle!
His brown face shone through its tears. Today he'd bought

paper and brushes and would paint it. We both
smiled, approving. He asked our names. I gave mine
'and this is Miranda.' He told us his

and asked would we please promise to say it
aloud somewhere so he'd know he was alive
outside his own self-knowledge. I said 'Tonight

I'll be in Paris. I'll say your name full voice
in the Marais, and even shout it: *"Freddy!"*'
Could that be right? It was the name he'd given.

Just like that

to Kevin Ireland

How handsome you were Kevin with all that hair
which mostly you've kept. We were Grammar boys,
soccer players for our schools' First Elevens
on opposite sides of the Harbour. Not friends
but with friends in common, and soon frequenters
of the Civic Wintergarden Cabaret,
ballroom dancers in the manner of the time,

waltz and foxtrot, samba, rumba and tango –
and poets, each of us now well on his way
to ninety and whatever end Fate chooses,
still teased, tormented, delighted by the play
of language, words in patterns on a page.
My recipe for long life? 'Peanut butter
and swimming', though my years on earth have been

curtailed I'm sure by smoking that has put
sclerotic arteries into battle with
a healthy pump. Also essential has been
an ally-partner – mine Kay as yours is Janet.
Swimming on my back at Kohimarama
I become again the connoisseur of clouds,
their feathery formations deftly painted

white against blue and nothing beyond except
infinity and the knowledge of Space and Time.
At Tohunga Crescent we can grow you grapes,
plums and flowers. Our cat's deep study of birds
is not encouraged. For me the aging prostate
makes peeing yet another matter of Time
and learning how much more there is to be seen

from a bathroom window, as now the sparrow
is doing his hummingbird hover over
the spider whose recent capture he'd like
to make his own; also the wax-eyes out there
are doing the bees' mahi in white blossom.
You're a luncher, Kevin, as I'm a dinner-man
but we meet whenever and wherever chance

and choice conjoin. The title poem you sent me
departed your kitchen, detoured at Esmond Road
then crossed the Harbour and flew right into mine –
'Just like that' you said, and here we are still
writing, almost ashamed to find ourselves
alive when so many worthy friends are not
with no excuse better than the clueless heart.

Sam

Sam
renegade rhymer
of the gravelly stammer
phones to say
it's a brain tumour
terminal
and that he's looking forward to
'the Great Journey';
that he loves us both
and
(Catholic to the quick)
'to that woman Kay
I genuflect'.

Lines for a
Granddaughter

When Gabriella
           about to marry Max
             asked for lines
to be read at their wedding
            what came to me
          was the sky at Kohi
blue
and its blueness more intense
      for the whiteness of clouds
escaped from their flock;

        and then again at night
that blue dissolved into darkness
pricked by stars.

               Lines
clumsy, uncertain, meandering –
           what was it
they wanted to say
      but that out of the chanciness
         of our pairings
      comes the hope for beauty
and that love may last?

Solidarity

Left alone with my friend Patsy's father
     while she dressed to go out
I was told he'd engendered three daughters
     with his just one testicle
a riding accident having cost him the other.

Were congrats in order?
     I settled for surprise
 and pleasure that Patsy had (so to speak)
'come through'.

    Later when I knew her better
I mentioned this revelation.
     It was news to her –
not the kind of thing you told a daughter
     in those far-off times
     but man-to-man
that was different.

Games at 14 Esmond Road, 1955

              In one we had to describe
our most interesting employment.

Mine was working on a walking-stick farm
              on the Canterbury Plains.
        The skill was to teach the canes
at a certain height to begin bending over
so they would grow a handle.

          Janet's was in a toothpaste factory
in deepest Penrose.
          She was in charge of the red stripe
          and had to get it into the white paste
             precisely so they would emerge
from the squeezed tube
together but distinct,
side by side.

        For that Frank awarded her First Prize
           though he said I had run her
a close second.

Thirteen Ways of Looking at Tony Rudolf

(and with Paula Rego)

1.
Euro-man
with tongues to match
and matchlessly
well-read

2.
poet
in the Stevens style
or the Williams way
but without the fans

3.
he looked with alarm
for bad things coming
as they sometimes were
indeed

4.
and sometimes not.
Was it he who
ate the oaks
on Woodside Ave?

5.
We'd disagreed
whether a Balzac story
had forecast
the art to come.

6.

My London lookout
in space and time
between the River
and the Hampstead Ponds

7.

he took me to the crematorium
at Golders Green
in search of fact
for my fiction *Risk.*

8.

I took him to Waikumete
and the grave of Jewish
Karl Wolfskehl
'Exul Poeta'.

9.

And don't forget the grandson
chess-playing Charlie –
and Katherine Mansfield
and Days Bay.

10.

In common we had
books, chess
a school with squash courts,
and circumcision.

11.

He was Paula's beautiful man
but in her 'Flight into Egypt'
subdued, dictated to
by the woman at his back.

12.

Remember the inn
Miranda
the high Pyrenees,
the teasy fleas and
the wine?

13.

Head full of heart
he gave her dying
the nightingale
and honeydew and
the milk of paradise.

$E = mc^2$

(in 13-syllable tercets)

Peter, Phil and
Treace – all Catholic
so they couldn't

enter a Protestant
church (old times!)
but came to our

wedding breakfast.
Phil went into the
army, Treace was

a Woolworths
manager, Peter a
teacher and then

a schools inspector.
Two at least I've
outlived. 'They were

my close companions
many a year'
says Yeats in that

contrived account
of Irish fame.
Symbols he should have

called them. Would
any of mine have
read John Berryman

who could have taught
them how to pray
to a God who's not

there but might
be that microwave
afterglow in space

recalling the Big
Bang? No Berryman
was not for

golfer Treace with his
handicap of one;
nor for Pete

who would have
preferred that
bleak old contemporary

Geoffrey Hill with his
'world spinning from
Jehovah's hand';

but might have
spoken to the
poet Phil was at heart.

Close companions
yes, but briefly –
symbols now and like

that glow of our
beginnings, lost in
deep space and time.

The Money

What do you make of one you knew
was 'a great man' whom everyone secretly knew
was not? – that was our friend Bill
who made a fortune and lost it
and not just once. It was not the fortune
(nor the loss either) made Bill great, but courage
cheerfully cooking stew for us when down
in his council flat, and when his luck was good
throwing reckless parties
in his plush harbour-side duplex.

But up or down there were always his stories
of movie stars and famous racing drivers
who'd been his friends
whose posters crammed his walls.

Impresario, journalist, producer
his first orgasm, he told us
had been at the hands
of a Marist Brother, his first wife
a Mary Quant model.

I met him in the pool at the Mortons'
tasty Murrays Bay house
on the North Shore. They were theatre people
and had a yacht slept four.
They never crashed like Bill, but still
their affluence all mysteriously leaked away.
Why were our favoured friends
unlucky when we were not, if it wasn't the caution
they lacked that made them lovely?

The Mortons live in deepest Verteillac now
freezing in the winters of rural France
but loved to bits by their neighbours.
Bill's in heaven driving a Porsche for God.

Ian

When my friend Ian crashed his Norton and died
I lay face-down gripping the grass with both hands
as if I thought I might fly off into space.

It was where we'd wrestled often in the night
after the pictures – a boys' ritual of pain
and strength and will. The adults spoke of his death

as 'tragedy' but showed no sign they felt it.
I thought my grief should be seen, pitied perhaps
but his sister Jean laughed at my long sad face.

Years later her daughter told me she'd hated him,
locking herself in their bathroom to escape
his angers. It's true he was strong, courageous,

a fighter with witty eyes, but a bully –
should I believe it? After seventy years
I might be the only person still alive

to remember you, Ian – so come with me now,
less a dark angel than an affable ghost.
Too late to make amends, too late for sorrow –

we'll go to the pictures (classic black-and-white
of the Forties) then ride your Norton much too fast
on Dominion Road, and wrestle into the night.

And last

We won't need to say goodbye
we've been saying it a lifetime
fond farewells – there had to be an end
and this will be it – goodbye loved friend
go well wherever
you can't travel without me
nor I without you
into that green world of neverforever
good books
good talk and swimming –
thankyou we say
from the heart I say it thankyou
meaning you
always.

Notes

Special acknowledgement and thanks to my fellow poet Alan Roddick who watched many of the poems in this collection through various stages of revision.

After receiving a cardiologist's prognosis that I would soon die I had intended to call this collection *Last Poems*, but it seemed the poem habit was so ingrained there was no 'last' as long as the brain went on working. Hence the quotation from Allen Curnow's poem about Mr Prisk the brick-maker: 'so long / as there's a next, there's no last' (see *What You Made of It*, 2021, pp. 226–27 for my exchange with Curnow about that poem). Alan Roddick uses the same quotation for the title of his most recent collection, *Next*.

Some of the poems in this collection were short-listed for the Otago University Press Kathleen Grattan Poetry Award in 2022. Locations where some have appeared include *Broadsheet*, *Ingenio*, *Yearbook: Katherine Mansfield Studies*, vol. 15 (ed. Gerri Kimber, Todd Martin & Aimée Gasston), *Landfall*, *Newsroom*, *NZ Review of Books*, *PN Review*, *Poetry New Zealand Yearbook 2020* (ed. Johanna Emeney), *New Zealand Listener*, *The Spinoff*, *The Ultimate Reader of Love for the Book* (ed. William Direen) and *Sylvia and the Birds* (ed. Johanna Emeney & Sarah Laing).

'Mary'
The whale came back next day and was identified by a person from Project Jonah as a young pygmy right whale – young because it was only about three metres in length while fully grown they are five. After that it was not seen again.

'Sonnet: Paula Rego and an inn'
The poem Paula Rego loved to hear us recite was 'Tarantella' by Hilaire Belloc ('Do you remember an inn, Miranda?'). The one who read it to her nightly was her partner Tony Rudolf.

'The thousand peaceful towns'

The poem I quoted was Verlaine's 'Mon rêve familier'. The trick for remembering the French words in which the 'l' was sounded as 'l' and not as 'y' was 'les mille villes tranquilles'.

Psalms of Judas, 1–4

In my novel *My Name Was Judas* (2006), Judas is a boyhood friend of Jesus and the only one among the disciples who is not able to believe in his divinity. He tries to save Jesus from the wrath of the Romans but fails. He is a poet and each of the chapters ends with a poem reflecting on the events that have taken place. These Psalms are more of his poems/reflections.

'For Jane Massey'

Daughter Margaret's London friend Jane was visiting Auckland when I blacked out swimming around the yellow buoy at Kohimarama. This poem in the Horatian manner uses the trope that a request for a poem for her fiftieth birthday had to be satisfied and so saved my life.

'Keri Hulme – *The Bone People*'

This, written on hearing of Keri's death, was one of those poems that seem to write themselves and leave the feeling that any revision would be an unwarranted interference. 'Bait' was the novel Keri was rumoured to have received an advance of £20,000 for and never produced. I thought I had read parts of it and that it was about a sort of ark in a time of flood, but when asked about it recently was not able to remember where, when or how I had seen it. 'Neuter' was the word Keri applied to her own sexuality.

'Crossing the Bar'

Ann Thwaite is the biographer of Emily Tennyson, Frances Hodgson Burnett, A. A. Milne and others. She spent part of her childhood in New Zealand – she and her brother sent out to stay with Kiwi relations when it seemed England was going to be invaded. She is my exact contemporary, hence the fantasy about the Mt Eden Pool where she records swimming as a child. Anthony was a significant poet, books editor for *The Listener* (BBC) and *The New Statesman*, poetry editor for Secker & Warburg, and possibly best known as Philip Larkin's literary executor and editor. They are old friends, and I borrowed two of their homes, The Mill House, Low Tharston in Norwich, and the one in Gloucester Terrace, London, for locations in two of my novels, *The Necessary Angel* (2018) and *Risk* (2012).

'Iris'
A truthful account – and Bayley had a prodigious stammer which was worst on the letters M and N, making his choice of subject for his lectures particularly unfortunate.

'Thirteen Ways of Looking at Tony Rudolf'
Anthony Rudolf, London poet and publisher, was the partner and principal male model of the Portuguese/British painter Dame Paula Rego during the last 25 years of her life. She died in June 2022.

'Ian'
I write about Ian Lamont and his death on pp. 212–14 of *South-West of Eden* (2009). The elegy I wrote for him is the earliest of my *Collected Poems* (2008).